THE Hudson

RIVER OF HISTORY

The Battle of Stony Point

THE
HUDSON
RIVER OF HISTORY

by May McNeer

GARRARD PUBLISHING COMPANY
CHAMPAIGN, ILLINOIS

THIS BOOK WAS EDITED AND DESIGNED
UNDER THE SUPERVISION OF NANCY LARRICK, ED.D.

The manuscript of this book was checked for
historical accuracy by Carl Carmer, author of
The Hudson in the Rivers of America series.

Copyright 1962 by May McNeer

View from a Staten Island ferry.   NYSPIX-Commerce

Contents

THE HUDSON RIVER VALLEY

Mt. MARCY

FORT TICONDEROGA

LAKE TEAR

HUDSON RIVER

LAKE GEORGE

A DIRONDACK MOUNTAINS

HUDSON FALLS

SACANDAGA RESERVOIR

HUDSON RIVER

MOHAWK

AMSTERDAM

RIVER

TROY

SCHENECTADY

ALBANY

HUDSON

NEW YORK

CATSKILL

CATSKILL MOUNTAINS

HUDSON RIVER

KINGSTON

POUGHKEEPSIE

NEWBURGH

STORM KING Mt.

WEST POINT

BEAR MOUNTAIN
STONY POINT

HAVERSTRAW

WHITE PLAINS

YONKERS

PALISADES

GEORGE WASHINGTON BRIDGE

THE BRONX

N

W   E

S

NEW JERSEY

NEWARK

JERSEY CITY

MANHATTAN

BROOK-LYN

QUEENS

NARROWS

STATEN ISLAND

SANDY HOOK

MASSACHUSETTS

WORCESTER

QUABBIN RESERVOIR

SPRINGFIELD

HARTFORD

CONNECTICUT

NEW LONDON

CANDLEWOOD LAKE

NEW HAVEN

DANBURY

BRIDGEPORT

LONG ISLAND SOUND

LONG ISLAND

ATLANTIC OCEAN

1. The Great River That Runs Two Ways

The Hudson River is famous for the beauty of its shores and for the vast depth of its ancient channel. It begins in tiny Lake Tear of the Clouds in the Adirondack Mountains of New York State. It runs for 315 miles from its source to the Atlantic Ocean. Lake Tear of the Clouds lies like a jewel on the slope of Mt. Marcy. Indians of that area called this high mountain the Cloud Splitter.

Joined by other streams and growing larger as it descends, it tumbles over rapids and falls. Then it becomes the main body of the Hudson River. Its largest tributary is the Mohawk River. This comes

7

From Bear Mountain the river winds through the Highlands.

into it from the west a few miles above Albany, the capital of New York. The Mohawk connects the Hudson Valley to the Finger Lake district of central New York.

The Hudson flows southward between low banks, then between gentle hills, and on past Albany. There the river is less than a quarter of a mile wide. Yet it is deep enough to permit some ocean-going vessels to come that far.

From Albany the river winds southward in large curves into the Catskill Mountains, where the Hudson Valley is called the Highlands. Here the river is most beautiful, swinging around sharp bends and points of land, or "hooks," as the Dutch spoke of them. Some of the highest rounded peaks are called Storm King, High Tor, Bear and Donderberg, or Thunder Mountain.

Below the mountains the river broadens until it looks like a series of lakes. The widest place is Haverstraw Bay, which is about three miles across. Tappan Zee, just below it, is almost as wide. Then the river flows south for about twenty miles, past Manhattan Island on the east, now the city of New York. On the west the Hudson washes New Jersey shores, where tall cliffs called the Palisades line the river banks. Here the Hudson is known as the North River, and it becomes part of the harbor of New York City.

Beneath the Hudson there is a great chasm, which grows deeper as it approaches the Atlantic Ocean. The melting of the last great ice covering in the Ice Age made this gorge under Hudson

9

waters. From the ocean nearly to Albany, the chasm floor is below sea level. This permits the salt ocean tides to ebb and flow as far as 150 miles up the river.

At the lower end of Manhattan Island, the Hudson joins the East River and other streams to form the Upper Bay of New York. From shore to shore this bay is about three miles wide. Then the river passes through a deep channel called the Narrows between the end of Long Island and Staten Island. Beyond the Narrows there is the Lower Bay, and then the Atlantic Ocean.

This very deep canyon under the water extends out into the ocean like a valley. It has a flat floor 30

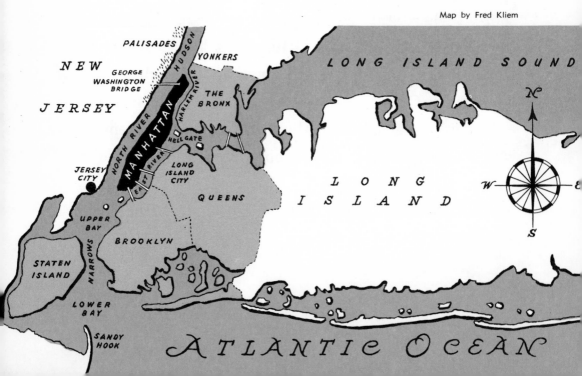

Map by Fred Kliem

The Palisades extend 20 miles along the New Jersey bank.

feet below the surface. Gradually it deepens to 3,600 feet under the ocean top. And, even beyond that point, the Hudson River channel makes still another drop called the "undersea falls." The bottom of the river canyon here lies 7,500 feet beneath the surface waves of the ocean.

Before the coming of the white man, the Hudson River and its valley belonged to different tribes of Indians. North of the Catskill Mountains the Iroquois claimed the region for their hunting grounds.

South of the Highlands a number of tribes pitched their grass and bark wigwams. Some were Algonkian speaking people, including the Delawares. They hunted in forests of huge trees, fished for shad in springtime and swam like otters in the river. They paddled their dugouts swiftly from shore to shore or walked over the ice in winter. The Manna-hatas on the eastern shore, and the Leni Lenape, a band of Delawares on the western side, were usually peaceable.

The name for the island of Manhattan, or Manna-hata, meant "Place of Beauty." Because the salt tides moved so far into the river course, Indians called the Hudson the "Great River That Runs Two Ways."

The first white men to enter the River That Runs Two Ways came in 1524. Their leader was Giovanni da Verrazano, who went no farther than the river mouth.

Henry Hudson, a British sea captain, was seeking a westward passage to China. In 1609 he sailed his little vessel, the *Half Moon,* into a river that he called the "Great River of the Mountains."

Henry Hudson's *Half Moon* was a sturdy little ship commissioned by the Dutch East India Company. It had a mixed crew of Dutch and English seamen.

Model of the Half Moon.

Captain Hudson looked with wonder at the river shores and at the many small islands in the harbor. Today some of these islands are called Staten Island, Governors Island, Ellis Island and Bedloe's or Liberty Island.

As the *Half Moon* swung at anchor near the island of the Manna-hatas, Indians wearing soft deerskin clothing paddled out from shore. Under the high prow of the vessel, they stood up in their canoes to offer gifts of fruits, corn and game. Captain Hudson welcomed the Indians aboard and gave them small gifts in return. Later he went ashore to a feast prepared for him. In his log he wrote that "the swarthy natives all stood and sang in their fashion among the great oaks."

Moving upstream, the *Half Moon* entered the Highlands region and sailed almost to the place where Albany, the capital of New York State, now stands. Here Hudson realized that he had not found the passage to the Orient, so he swung the little ship around and sailed back down the river.

As the *Half Moon* lay at anchor one night, an Indian brought his canoe alongside and climbed in

14

This old print shows Indians paddling out to meet the Half Moon.

through an open porthole. A little later he let himself down into his canoe again carrying several stolen articles. The first mate thought that he saw

The Museum of the City of New York displays this scale model showing the Half Moon *as it came into New York harbor in 1609.*

something move. A blast of his gun shattered the quiet, and the Indian brave fell from his canoe.

All night the crew waited and watched, guns ready. As the sun rose on a brilliant October day, Indian war canoes came in on all sides of the *Half Moon.* Arrows whizzed on deck from dugouts steered expertly by painted warriors. Several sailors were killed as they fired their muskets at the swiftly advancing and retreating canoes.

Captain Hudson set sail at once. As the *Half Moon* rounded a curve of the river, it passed under a jutting cliff. From the rocky top nearly a hundred Indians braves sent a storm of arrows down on the decks. Keeping to the middle of the stream, the *Half Moon* reached the harbor. Then she headed for the open sea. At last, she sailed into a safe port in the Netherlands. Since Hudson was employed by the Dutch, his discovery was claimed by them as their property.

Henry Hudson never came back to his great river. But years later the English named the mighty stream for him. Captain Hudson could not have dreamed that someday the richest city on earth would be built on the Hudson River.

2. In the Days of the Dutch

For fifteen years after the *Half Moon* had disappeared over the eastern horizon, the Great River That Runs Two Ways belonged only to the Indians. During those years, a few of the strange men with pale skins came up river and built a tiny log fort for fur trading. They called the place Fort Nassau. After a short time they left the fort and sailed away across the ocean.

One day in the year 1623, Indians saw another ship in the river. This vessel was anchored off the green island of the Manna-hatas. On the decks of the ship, the *New Netherlands*, men, women and children crowded the rails to gaze at the pleasant shores.

18

They talked excitedly in French. They were Protestant Walloons who were fleeing from the Spanish Netherlands to escape persecution because of their religious beliefs.

Each newly arriving group of people gave the river a new name. The Walloons called it the Mauritius River, in honor of their ruler, Maurice, the Prince of Orange. Some of the farmers traveled north to the Fresh River, later called the Connecticut. Others went south to the Delaware River. Only a few stayed on Manhattan Island at the river's mouth.

Eighteen families on board the *New Netherlands* sailed through the Highlands and on to old Fort Nassau. A few miles above this ruin, they went ashore on the western bank to build Fort Orange on a hill near the river.

Although the soil was rich, farming did not flourish. The Walloons found it easier and more profitable to trade with the Indians. A few trinkets would buy valuable furs.

During the next few years men from the Netherlands, France, England, Ireland, Scotland and Germany joined the Walloons, both at Fort Orange and on Manhattan Island.

The Dutch government wanted farmers in the valley. But as soon as farmers arrived, they gave up the hard work of clearing fields for farm land and began to trade for fox and beaver pelts. To encourage farming, domestic animals were sent over in three ships named the *Horse*, the *Sheep* and the *Cow*. But this made no difference to the people.

After a few years the beaver pelt was so valuable that it served for money. Goods were reckoned as worth so many skins.

Yet the Dutch government in the motherland wanted to hold this territory. In order to encourage farming, the government gave large tracts of land in the Hudson Valley to a few rich Dutchmen. These landholders were called *patroons*. They could get tenants, who could not afford to buy land, to live there and farm the estates. In return, each year the tenant farmers paid for using the land. As rent they turned over a large part of their grain and other farm products, as well as all of their new-born livestock. Governing these great areas was left to this handful of wealthy Dutch patroons.

One of these patroons was Kiliaen Van Rensselaer, a wealthy jeweler in Holland. He did not come to America himself, but he sent out a manager for his enormous estate. Van Rensselaer owned land on both sides of the Hudson near Fort Orange, now Albany. His sons came over to make their home on the Hudson. They ruled like kings without opposition. Their palatial home was called "Rensselaerswyck."

For two hundred years the patroon system continued in the Hudson Valley. It made the landlords rich and kept tenant farmers poor.

In 1626 Peter Minuit came from Holland as the first Director General of the colony of New Netherland. New Amsterdam was the one settlement of importance in the colony. Protecting its narrow dwellings, gardens and windmills, was a wooden fort on a hill. A wall made of upright logs was built along the north end of town. Beyond there were farms already being cut out of the forest.

One day Peter Minuit called together the chiefs of the small wandering Indian bands that had always

Museum model showing Peter Minuit bargaining with the Indians.

come and gone as they wished on the island. They stood beneath a tall tree and made a bargain with Minuit. The oldest known manuscript telling the history of New Amsterdam recorded the event.

The old chief spoke up for his people's rights.

"We have talked in council. We will take your gifts and let you dwell on the island of the Manna-hatas. We will come and go. We will raise our lodges. We will hunt as we have always done."

The sun glanced down on the Director General's Dutch clothing and gleamed on the silver buckles of his shoes. He spoke to the chiefs and their warriors. Then he had gifts brought to delight the

22

Indians. The gifts were knives, metal pots, beads and cloth worth sixty guilders, or about twenty-four dollars.

On the island of Manhattan the tiny Dutch settlement of New Amsterdam grew rapidly. Dutch merchants, or burghers, lived there with their stout wives, sons and daughters. In their steep-roofed stone houses, they enjoyed a comfortable life with a great deal to eat and drink. The housewives, or *vrows*, scrubbed, cooked and gossiped all day with their neighbors. At the end of the day, their men folk returned home to smoke their long-stemmed pipes.

In the seventeenth century, New Amsterdam was

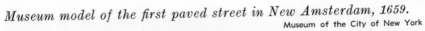

Museum model of the first paved street in New Amsterdam, 1659.

not all Dutch. Traders from New England journeyed overland to the Hudson and back. Ships came in from other parts of the world too. Sailors from many countries came ashore to buy and sell goods of every description. Many of these things were smuggled in under the very noses of the inspectors. Dutch merchants dealt with smugglers daily.

For lack of other amusement, Dutchmen played practical jokes on each other. One evening the town trumpeter, Antony Van Corlaer, stepped up to a friend's ear and blew a great blast on his trumpet. Antony the joker carried a black eye and bruises for many a day thereafter. Even worse for him, huge gusts of laughter rolled about whenever he appeared.

These Dutchmen were quarrelsome, too, and were often in court for bedeviling their neighbors. They would also report their friends for annoying them. Even the pastors, delivering sermons that threatened fire and brimstone, were rebuked by them. When Dominie Bogardus bore down on the town fathers for their sins, these gentlemen ordered every bell in town to be rung. They also sent a band to play loudly in front of the church to drown out the Dominie's sermons.

☆ ☆ ☆

In the years after Minuit made his bargain with the Indians, independent Dutch farmers took land for themselves across the river in Nova Caesarea, now New Jersey. They cleared their fields and put up redstone houses and barns. Above Manhattan Island, on the eastern shore, more patroons settled. They took far more land than they were supposed to have. But the governors who followed Minuit made no attempt to stop them.

In 1646, Peter Stuyvesant became Director General, or Governor, of New Netherland. He had no sooner arrived, than he heard that Van Rensselaer's manager, Crol, was stealing land from the colony. Tenant farmers called Crol the Old Gray Thief. Stuyvesant had been sent by the Dutch West India Company, which then ran the colony. He was also an honest man and decided to go after Crol. Stumping along on his wooden leg, Stuyvesant went up the gangplank of a river sailing sloop. Behind him came a company of soldiers. They headed up river to find the Old Gray Thief.

As the ship came to Fort Orange, Stuyvesant could see the log fort with the flag of the colony flying on it. But around the fort, outside of its outer walls, Crol was putting up buildings for Van Rensselaer. Stuyvesant's lean face flushed with rage. He climbed nimbly enough over the ship's side and into a small boat. As he came in to shore, he roared out orders to his troops, who were right behind him.

"Lower that flag!"

The Old Gray Thief scowled, but he could not resist the Governor. Peg-Leg Peter marked out the boundaries of company land and called it Beverwyck. He set up a government to keep in check both the wild frontiersmen and the patroons.

For years hundreds of white sails gleamed on the Hudson River until ice and snow put them into winter docks. The sloops were gaily painted in red, blue and yellow.

These Hudson sloops were designed especially for

26

Peter Stuyvesant, Governor of New Netherland.

this river. Each one was usually about seventy feet long, and had a high, rounded prow. Its tall mast made it look top-heavy. Yet the Dutch sloop was a fine vessel for the deep winding river, where winds were often changeable.

Skippers on these ships were Hollanders, but they knew every point and hook, every kind of wind, and how the tides affected the river. The sailors spoke many languages, but the speech of Holland was heard most often. Sometimes a sloop would have a crew of Negro slaves, all talking in Dutch.

When a merchant in New Amsterdam went on board, he was ready for a long voyage. His friends came to see him off as if he were going across the Atlantic Ocean.

Passengers enjoyed listening to the captain of a sloop. A river Dutchman could tell a fanciful tale about every landmark around Manhattan Island and on the entire length of the Hudson River. The skipper could also make imaginary elves and goblins of the valley seem as much alive as the crew.

"Mynheer, you know Hell Gate—where East River water boils over the rocks? Never go on that water

At the new Tappan Zee bridge, the river is almost three miles wide.

when the night is dark and the wind is blowing up a storm! Never do it, Mynheer. For then the Black Pirate Spook, who was killed by Peg-Leg Peter—he will run you down with his boat. The Hudson is safer than that, Mynheer. On the shore of Manhattan Island, on a stormy night, many have heard the Spook rowing back and forth with muffled oars."

As a skipper sailed his sloop onto the waters of wide Tappan Zee, he was afraid that he might catch a glimpse of a ghost ship. There were many stories about the Stormship of the Palisades. It was said to

29

shift like a wisp of gray fog back and forth between the shores sometimes. A sight of it told the captain that a gale would blow up before morning.

The Hudson River sloops sailed up the river past Anthony's Nose and Storm King Mountain. This was the region of those magical "little men of the Highlands." They were supposed to dress in wide Dutch breeches, leather doublets and high-crowned hats. According to the tales, the little men of the Highlands liked to bowl. As they knocked down the pins, thunder rolled over the river.

When a sloop rounded the bend under Donderberg Mountain, the captain would roar out a command to lower the peak sail. This was the home of a goblin called the Heer. Unless he was greeted politely, he might send down a storm to sink the ship. Some who claimed to have seen him said that the Heer wore a hat shaped like a loaf of sugar. When he shouted into his speaking trumpet in Dutch, deep thunder bounced from one mountainside to another, and lightning flashed from shore to shore.

As a ship sailed toward the village of Catskill, passengers could look up at the mountains rising

The Heer of Donderberg Mountain.
Drawing by Aldren Watson

behind it. Here Rip Van Winkle went to sleep with his hungry dog beside him, and awoke to play at bowls with the little men of the Highlands. And, there, on that road winding down into the village, one could almost see old Rip coming back a generation later, at the end of his long nap.

Other vessels not so gay moved in and out of New Amsterdam harbor. These were run by smugglers, who brought in goods from every part of the world. They refused to pay government taxes on goods. Time after time armed officers were sent out to catch smuggling ships. But smugglers knew how to slip in and out like shadows. They left rich cargoes in hidden places on shore, to be picked up by small boats and delivered to the town after dark. In New Amsterdam one could buy anything from furs to jewels, good woolen cloth, spices and tea—all smuggled in by daredevil crews.

Sometimes even the company running the colony had ships that were used for secret smuggling. Furs were sent out for goods brought in. Beaver pelts were the most profitable.

During warm months, village people in the river

valley were used to the sight of Indians trading pelts for goods. Often beaver skins were swapped for sweet Dutch cookies and cakes. The Indians liked these cookies so much that for a while there were laws forbidding their sale to the braves and squaws. Too many Indians in town seemed dangerous.

Wampum was used as money by all the tribes. But the Indians never were able to make enough for themselves. So Dutchmen began to make the little beads out of purple and white clam shells. Before long hundreds of village and farm homes all up and down the river were called "wampum shops." Women and children became as skilled as their menfolk in making wampum.

Along the Hudson River, Indians were peaceable until they were cheated or treated cruelly. Then they went to war, burned farms and killed settlers. After some years Indians of the lower Hudson River country had to move away to more distant forests and streams. When the Dutch rule on the Hudson came to an end, only the fierce Iroquois remained. They still believed that they could hold their hunting grounds by force of arms.

3.   A Royal Gift of a River

Governor Peter Stuyvesant planted his peg leg firmly on top of the flat roof of the fort in New Amsterdam. Through his spyglass he gazed at the British fleet in the distant harbor.

This was the year 1664. The British lion had his mighty paw on Peter Stuyvesant's colony. The British king, Charles the Second, had decided that the Dutch colony belonged to him. Furthermore, he had just given it to his brother James, Duke of York. The Duke's ships had come to take the colony.

All morning Stuyvesant's men could hear the thump-thump-thump of Peter's wooden leg as he paced the roof. When they heard him coming down the steps, every tap sounded sad. The soldiers knew what that meant.

Already Connecticut had been taken by the English-speaking Yankees. Next day the British came in to New Amsterdam. They left with the surrender paper signed in the cramped hand of Peter Stuyvesant.

When British officers arrived to take over the colony, they found Stuyvesant dressed in his full uniform, cocked hat and sword. He believed that he had made good terms for his people. They could keep their property, and they would still have trading rights with the Dutch.

New Amsterdam became New York, and Beverwyck was named Albany. The Mauritius River was now the Hudson River.

The Dutch continued to use their own language. They also kept their customs and their fanciful tales of ghosts and goblins.

Washington Irving, a New York author, put many of these tales into his writings. He wrote the story of old Rip Van Winkle. He also published his amusing *Knickerbocker's History of New York*.

One of his stories tells how Harlem Creek came to be called Spuyten Duyvil at the place where it meets the Hudson River. When the British were threatening the city, Antony Van Corlear, the trumpeter, was sent by Stuyvesant to rouse the countryside. At Harlem Creek water spurts high over the rocks. When Antony reached this point, he tried to cross.

People heard him blowing his trumpet. They said that they saw the devil rise from the foaming waves and grab Antony by a sturdy leg. With a loud blast on his trumpet, he went under, never to be seen again. Ever since, this spot has been called Spuyten Duyvil which means "Spouting Devil." This is where Harlem Creek makes Manhattan an island.

Peter Stuyvesant left his town house and retired to his farm or *bouwerie*. This is where the street called the Bowery now runs. There he lived in the good old Dutch manner, eating and drinking with neighbors on every feast day. In the evening he sat under his pear tree and smoked a pipe. When he died, Stuyvesant was buried in a chapel later called St. Mark's-in-the-Bowery.

Drawing by Aldren Watson

They say the devil rose from the waves and pulled Antony under.

For a long time "Peter's Pear Tree" shaded his old home. And for a long time New York folk with Dutch names said they could hear a distinct thump-thumping on a dark night. This was the ghost of Peg-Leg Peter, watching over his people.

The Dutch soon adjusted to British rule. They found that they had no more to complain about than before the English came. They still hated taxes on goods. That problem they solved, however, as they had done before. They continued to smuggle goods in and beaver and other pelts out of the colony.

A great quarrel sprang up over the ownership of Staten Island, the largest of the harbor islands. Both New York and New Jersey claimed it. Legend has it that the Duke of York settled the dispute.

"An island that can be circumnavigated in twenty-four hours belongs to me," declared the King's brother. Nobody knew how he came to that decision, but nobody wanted to dispute him.

"Call in Captain Billop. There is a man who can sail around Staten Island."

Captain Billop came, nodded and said he "thought he might." He went back to his ship, the *Bentley*. He decided that if he placed rows of empty barrels on deck, they would catch the breeze and help his sails to speed him on his way. As the sun rose, a throng gathered on the shores of the river where it met the bay. The *Bentley* caught a fair breeze in her sails and in her barrels. Smoothly she moved out of sight beyond the green hills of Staten Island.

In just over twenty-three hours, the little *Bentley* rounded the last point. Staten Island became part of New York, although it is closer to New Jersey.

Today railroads and highways follow the shores of the river.

In those days there were many sawmills on the streams pouring into the Hudson north of the Highlands. In spring the mills sent floods of logs floating down. These were joined together to make huge rafts. On the rafts, loggers and their families built shacks and took a trip down the Hudson River to New York, tending the logs as they traveled. There they boarded the sloops for a slow sail homeward.

Sloop captains were still masters of the river. They took produce and passengers down to the city, and brought back money or purchases for them.

As a boat moved down river, passengers could see

the mansions of patroons and English landlords on many of the high points above the river. Along the Hudson, many wealthy English families had settled among the Dutch, and the English language was usually spoken. Palatial homes of the landowners were built like royal mansions in Persia, Germany, Italy or Greece. All had acres of gardens, and some had ruins imported from Europe to make the Hudson area look ancient.

For 200 years tenant farmers did not own land in the Hudson Valley. Each of their revolts was put down. But in a few years there was always another.

One day a quiet young Irish farmer named Prendergast and his Quaker wife rode through Westchester calling farmers out to join their rebellion. Tenants dropped their plows and scythes and followed. First, they marched to the house of a judge who had ousted many farmers from their homes for not paying rent to the patroon. They ducked the judge in his own duck pond.

Then they went from farm to farm, throwing out new farmers who had moved in when the original tenants were ousted by the judge.

At last Prendergast decided to take his men to New York City. As they marched, they shouted, "We are free men! Give us our rights!"

In the city the British General Gage called up every soldier. Terrified citizens locked themselves indoors. They knew that Prendergast had more than a thousand angry farmers in his "army." They knew, also, that up river more farmers were joining the revolt.

Then Prendergast received a message saying that General Gage was sending a regiment of Grenadiers to the countryside. The farmers knew they could not fight trained soldiers. Most of them went back home. Only 500 remained with Prendergast and his wife.

When Prendergast surrendered, his wife rode to the governor to ask for mercy for her husband. At the governor's request, the English king pardoned Prendergast.

The rebellion was over. But the patroons were still in control.

In Tarrytown, the great patroon Frederic Philipse lived well in his big castle. Philipse Castle was a

Part of the Philipse Castle as it appears today.

complete world in itself. There were barns, wind-mills, storehouses and dwellings—everything needed for a small kingdom.

Philipse Castle still stands in Tarrytown. It has been rebuilt so that visitors may see it as it was in patroon times.

☆ ☆ ☆

In the late eighteenth century, New York City was growing beyond the bounds of a Dutch town. It was noisy and busy, especially along the wharves.

The harbor was crowded with vessels. Some of these ships were welcome but some were not. Pirate ships still invaded the Hudson River as they did in early days.

Most of the pirates had their home bases off the coast of Florida, the Carolinas or New England. But they often came in and out of New York. Some even walked the streets of the city as if they owned the place.

The most famous pirate of them all was bold Captain William Kidd. He came into the city like any quiet citizen, making no attempt to disguise himself.

Kidd had first been hired to capture pirate ships. But it wasn't long before he was known as the terror of the Spanish Main. He owned a house on Wall Street, where his respectable wife lived.

Finally Captain Kidd was captured in New York City and sent to England. There he was tried and hanged. Later a popular ballad was written about the buccaneer.

My name was Captain Kidd when I sailed,
when I sailed.
My name was Captain Kidd when I sailed.
My name was Captain Kidd.
God's laws I did forbid.
And so wickedly I did when I sailed.

On the Hudson River one of the favorite legends is about the bold pirate captain. For two centuries treasure hunters have dug for his gold without finding any of it. Some say that the wild spirit of that bloodthirsty buccaneer guards it with cutlass in hand. It is even said that just one glimpse of the fearsome phantom can blind a treasure hunter for life.

In 1699 British warships anchored at Sandy Hook, outside of New York harbor. They intercepted pirate ships and cleared the port. Yet for the next hundred years, pirate ships hid in lonely coves and bays along the coasts. The pirates waited to sail out and board a ship going into the port on the Hudson River.

Although the colonists feared pirates, not many were the victims of pirates. By 1750 most Americans were more worried about their British rulers. Many felt they were being treated unfairly by their mother country and its king.

4. War on the River

TAXES! Taxes on stamps. Taxes on tea. Taxes on imported goods coming into the Hudson Valley. Unjust taxes!

"We did not make the laws of England. They gave us no voice in the government. Taxes keep us poor," shouted the colonists.

People gathered in villages and towns to talk about taxes and to disagree. They argued on country roads when one farmer met another. Some colonists wanted to be free of England. They became known as Patriots or Continentals. Others, loyal to England, were called Loyalists or Tories.

In New York the settlers disagreed also. There

was a riot in the streets in 1770. British redcoats marched to Golden Hill to break up a meeting of the Sons of Liberty. Soldiers with drawn swords drove away the angry stone-throwing colonists.

In 1774 New York Patriots had their own "Tea Party." They rushed the gangplank of the ship *London*, moored in the North River. Finding boxes of tea in the hold, they brought them to the deck and threw them overboard. As the tea floated down the river, the Patriots shouted defiance of British tax laws.

In April, 1775, news of the Battle of Lexington and Concord came from Boston. Then the men of the Hudson Valley knew they must prepare for war.

The mighty Hudson River was important to the British. If they could hold it, they could cut the the northern colonies off from those to the south. The Hudson was so important to both sides that it was called the "Key of the Revolution."

Soon the Hudson River was hemmed in by the British in the north. There they held Fort Ticonderoga on Lake Champlain. They were also friendly with the fierce Iroquois tribes.

In 1776 a British fleet sailed into the harbor of New York. Loyalists cheered as they saw war ships sailing up to anchor under the steep Palisades.

"Redcoats are on Staten Island!" they shouted.

"Yes," cried the Patriots, "but General Washington is on Long Island!"

All along the river valley, Patriot farmers left their homes to join the army of huge George Clinton, who was a farmer's son himself. Clinton gathered a rough but determined army. He intended to fortify islands in the Highlands region and strengthen tiny log forts already on the river banks.

The hot month of August, 1776, was eventful on the Hudson. American seamen were making fire ships to launch an attack on the British fleet as it came up the river. These fire ships would be set ablaze and rammed into the enemy ships. The men aboard knew their mission might result in death.

The attack failed as a battle. But one fire ship destroyed the English sloop *Carlotta* in the Tappan Zee. Valiant Ensign Thomas died in the attack. This stirred Americans from the harbor Narrows to the foothills of the Adirondacks.

On the night of August 17, a little band of men landed secretly on Governors Island off the tip of Manhattan Island. They were preparing the strangest attack of the war.

David Bushnell was in charge. He directed the launching of a craft which he had invented and called the *Turtle*. His navigator was Sergeant Ezra Lee of the Continental Army.

The *Turtle* was the first practical working submarine in history. Bushnell said it looked like a "hard-shell clam wearing a hat." Ezra Lee crawled

This old drawing gives an underwater view of Bushnell's submarine.

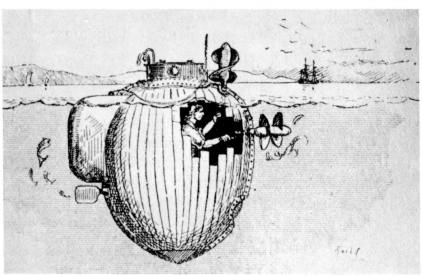

In this old painting you see the Turtle *approaching the British ship* Eagle.

into his small hole in the middle of the wooden frame. He pulled down the watertight domed cover, which moved on hinges. A whaleboat towed the *Turtle* out into the choppy waters of the harbor, as near the British fleet as possible.

The *Turtle* submerged. Lee could steer it easily backward and forward at a speed of three miles an hour. He could rise to the surface when he wished. Hitched behind the *Turtle* was an egg-shaped weapon filled with gunpowder.

Lee moved his submarine closer to the fleet and

prepared to fire his weapon. Then a lookout on the British ship *Eagle* saw the moon gleaming on a queer, rounded object. He raised an alarm. Lee headed for Manhattan Island, where his ship was captured.

Although the submarine proved useless to the Continentals, General Washington called the invention "an effort of genius."

The tall General who led the rebellious colonists had reason to remember that month of August. His forces were fewer than those of the British who opposed him in the Battle of Long Island. Many of his regiments were poorly trained.

Washington had to withdraw to New York and then march his army to the Battle of Harlem Heights. General Clinton brought his Hudson Valley boys to join Washington at the Battle of White Plains. But the Continentals had to retreat, and Washington's army withdrew across Manhattan.

Then the General took his men across the Hudson River to Fort Lee, which was perched on the top of the Palisades in New Jersey. There the troops began to strengthen the fort as fast as they could.

Map by Fred Kliem

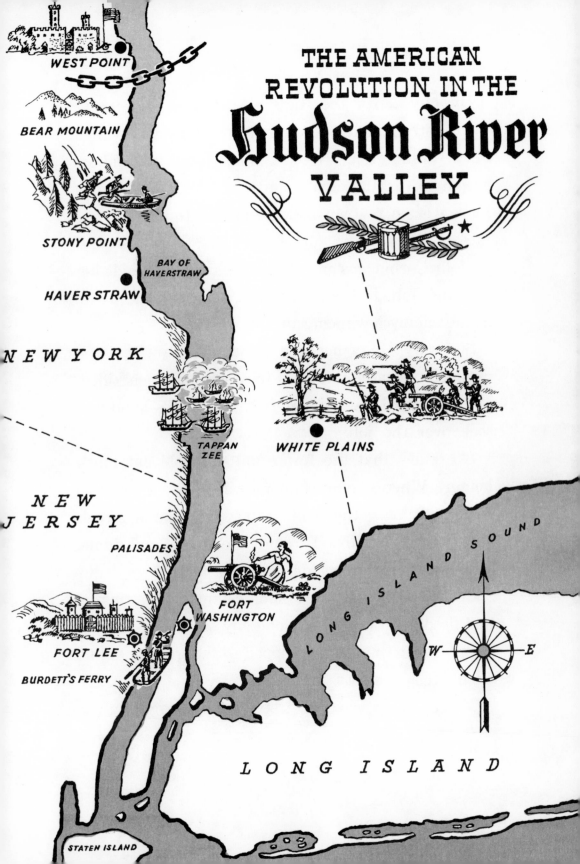

THE AMERICAN REVOLUTION IN THE
Hudson River
VALLEY

WEST POINT

BEAR MOUNTAIN

STONY POINT

BAY OF HAVERSTRAW

HAVER STRAW

NEW YORK

TAPPAN ZEE

WHITE PLAINS

NEW JERSEY

PALISADES

FORT WASHINGTON

FORT LEE

BURDETT'S FERRY

LONG ISLAND SOUND

LONG ISLAND

STATEN ISLAND

W — E

Directly across the Hudson from Fort Lee, there was a stronghold on Manhattan. This was called Fort Washington. Here a small band of soldiers prepared for the British attack. With these men there were a few wives, who refused to leave in the face of danger.

Molly Corbin was one of these. She stood beside her husband John, whose cannon fired again and again at the enemy advancing up the hill.

Suddenly Molly heard a shout. The gunner who rammed the cannon muzzle for John had been killed. Molly grasped the rammer from the man's hand and took over the job.

She knew that the fort could not hold out much longer. When enemy cannons were close enough to send balls over the wall, a burst of flame struck with a roar near by. Through the smoke and flame, Molly saw John lying dead at her feet.

She sprang to the cannon, rammed the muzzle, and fired over and over. Suddenly she felt a searing pain. Unconscious, she dropped to the ground as the enemy took the fort.

Molly Corbin was the first woman to fight in the

war. People called her "Captain Molly." For the rest of her life she wore the coat of an artilleryman.

Beneath the cliff at Fort Lee, Burdett's Ferry also played an important part in the war. Burdett was a Patriot. He had several boats moving day and night to bring Washington's troops over to Fort Lee. He rowed the General and his officers to the middle of the river to watch the Battle of Fort Washington. Then he brought them quickly back, to make hasty plans for retreat. Everyone knew that the much larger British Army would climb the Palisades before long. They knew that Fort Lee could not be held.

General Washington led his weary, discouraged men in a long line down the western slope of the Palisades. They moved across the salt meadows to Hackensack. The men were loaded with all the supplies they could carry. The rest they had had to leave behind. From time to time they stopped to fight skirmishes with British scouts and Loyalists.

With the Patriots was a man named Thomas Paine. He was not a soldier. He was a writer whose pamphlets had stirred the whole thirteen colonies to rebellion. As he walked down the rough wagon road, he thought of another pamphlet. Then he sat down beside the campfire at night and wrote it on the head of a drum. The pamphlet was called *The Crisis*. It began with words forever remembered in America:

"These are the times that try men's souls. The summer soldier and the sunshine patriot will, in this crisis, shrink from the service of his country; but he that stands it NOW, deserves the love and thanks of man and woman."

Washington's men left the Hudson and moved on to winter quarters at Valley Forge, Pennsylvania. Yet the war continued in the valley of the Great River of the Mountains.

Years before, iron forges had been set up at several places in New Jersey. At one of them men were working at top speed to complete a huge iron chain. At night the chain was carted in pieces, by wagon, to the Hudson. There, at the riverside, it was put together secretly. Then its enormous links were drawn across the river and fastened below West Point.

Patriots smiled grimly, "That will hold the King's

warships. They'll not get past that chain into the upper valley!"

Of all the points on the river, West Point was the most important to hold. And it was the best place for a fort. Two years after the fall of Fort Lee, the British were holding both sides of the lower Hudson. Yet Americans were still in control above the Bay of Haverstraw and the Tappan Zee.

Thaddeus Kosciusko, the famous Polish builder who believed in freedom, supervised the construction of a stronghold at West Point. A year later General Washington returned to make it his headquarters.

United States Military Academy at West Point as it looks today.

New York State Department of Commerce

Big George Clinton was still on the upper river. He was using his troops to build forts and defend the valley. Now, to the dismay of the Loyalists, some of the most powerful men of the Hudson area were aiding the Continental cause. Robert Livingston was one of them, along with Van Rensselaer. So was Peter Schuyler. He not only gave supplies and money, but also led troops from Albany to join Washington's forces.

The British were determined to control the entire Hudson. Redcoats and Hessians commanded by General Burgoyne marched into the upper region of the river. Now the river valley was in the most dangerous position of the entire war. In New York City, British troops prepared to go up the river.

The Patriots tried to hold Burgoyne's army in the north. The Americans, commanded by General Gates, met Burgoyne's British, Hessian and Iroquois Indian soldiers at Saratoga, in northern New York. After a fierce battle, the Continentals defeated the British, who surrendered on October 17, 1777. The hero of Saratoga was Benedict Arnold, whose leg was shot off in the field.

At West Point part of Washington's Great Chain is on display.

The Battle of Saratoga was the turning point in the war along the Hudson. Patriots from New England to Georgia celebrated the news of the American victory. Now that the British could not control the north, they must also be driven out of the lower Hudson region! Now they would be held off by that great chain that stretched across the river!

Everybody believed that the chain would hold. Yet when the British fleet came up the river, Patriots heard the loud clank of tools on iron. They watched

57

British Navy men remove the chain and sail their ships on up the Hudson.

The Americans were not only fighting the British— they had to fight the Loyalists and their friends, the Iroquois Indians. In 1778, stories of Indian massacres began to be heard along the Hudson. The Loyalists and Iroquois were burning, killing and destroying along the Mohawk River. Soon they would be spreading destruction into the Hudson Valley too.

General Washington sent an army to stop the Iroquois. In the next year there was great rejoicing among the Hudson Valley settlers, for the Indian towns were destroyed. The Iroquois were no longer able to help the British fight.

Americans were grim, hungry and weary in 1779. Yet they could still see the funny side of some events on the river. When British troops landed at Stony Point, and advanced on the two American forts north of it on the western side of the Hudson, General George Clinton was at one of them. He did not believe that Fort Montgomery and Fort Clinton could be taken easily, although the holding forces were not large. Yet, when the redcoats arrived at Stony Point, they advanced quickly on the forts, for a Tory farmer showed them the way. A sharp battle was fought bravely by Continental soldiers, but it was soon over. General Clinton, who was now the elected governor of New York State as well, had to order a hasty retreat. Some of the Americans disappeared into the woods, but others made for small boats waiting for them on the river.

The General slid down a cliff with great speed. Up and down the valley people laughed when they

General Anthony Wayne attacked the British at Stony Point.

told how the slide had cost him the seat of his trousers.

As the war moved from the Hudson Valley, New York City was still held by the enemy. A British fleet remained in the North River, but West Point was still held by Americans.

On a dark night in 1780 a British warship, the *Vulture*, moved quietly up the Hudson. A slender man wrapped in a greatcoat was put ashore from the British vessel. He landed a few miles below West Point. Another dim figure advanced to clasp hands with him. The two men talked until dawn. The *Vulture* lay in ghostly silence.

When daylight came, the British major, John André, had complete plans of the West Point fortifications. They were given to him by General Benedict Arnold, American hero of the Battle of Saratoga.

Major André was stepping into a small boat when Americans on the opposite shore fired at the *Vulture*. Without waiting for the Major, the warship weighed anchor and sailed down river. All that André could do was to hide in the nearby home of a Loyalist.

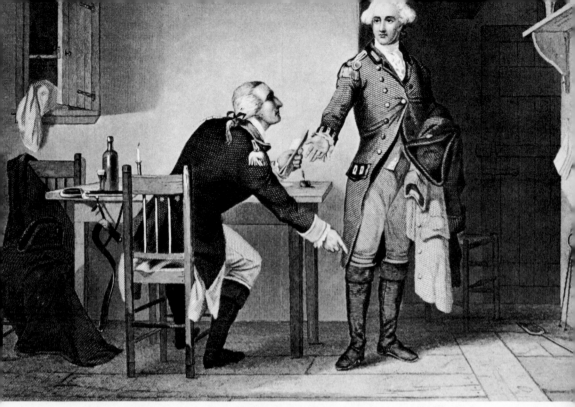

Arnold, with papers in hand, suggests hiding them in André's boot.

General Arnold returned secretly to West Point. After dark, André was rowed across the river and then supplied with a horse. He thought himself safe as he approached Tarrytown. And then, near Sleepy Hollow churchyard, he was hailed by three Continental soldiers. They searched him and found the plans for West Point hidden in the Major's boot. They could hardly believe their eyes.

Major John André was tried as a spy, found guilty and hanged in Tappan, New York. But Benedict

Arnold escaped on the *Vulture*. His name has meant "treason" to America ever since that day.

By now fighting was about over along Hudson shores. When Cornwallis surrendered at Yorktown, Virginia, great bonfires flamed up on the high bluffs of the Hudson. Jubilant Patriots shouted and danced like Indians. Horsemen galloped along country roads with the news.

While peace was being settled by the statesmen, General Washington and his staff lived on the Hudson, not far from Newburgh. In November, 1783, the British embarked for the last time from New

General Washington bade farewell to his officers at Fraunces Tavern.

*Fraunces
Tavern
today*

Courtesy Sons of the Revolution in the State of New York,
Headquarters, Fraunces Tavern, New York City

York City. Washington led his troops to Manhattan Island. In Fraunces Tavern, he spoke his farewell message to his army, with his officers around him. Then he crossed the wide gray waters of the Hudson to return to his home in Virginia.

As his boat pulled slowly away from the New York shore, a great crowd cheered him. He landed under the overhanging cliffs of New Jersey. There small Dutch towns looked down on this final scene of the American Revolution on the river.

The Clermont *on its first trip.*

5. Valley of the Hudson

One day in August, 1807, the white-capped waters of the Hudson River were alive with excitement. Sails dipped and billowed, and small craft of every kind cluttered the channel. On shore a vast crowd jeered at an awkward vessel beside a wharf on the New York waterfront.

"Look there! Why, it is Mr. Robert Livingston risking his life on that freak!"

"Why not? They say his money built her."

The gangplank was crowded with important people going on board the *Clermont*, nicknamed "Fulton's Folly." This was the first steamboat to try a real voyage.

"There's Robert Fulton, the inventor, standing by

Mr. Livingston's daughter, Harriet."

"He didn't invent the steamboat. I saw the little *Juliana* cross the river three years ago. And Fitch had one of those silly things on Collect Pond. It looks like a teakettle."

"Teakettle, is it? Looks more like the devil going up river in a sawmill."

Nobody expected the thing to run. Then in went the gangplank and up came the steam. The crowd pulled back fearfully as side paddles churned water all over the gay passengers. On an open deck they could see the engine and boiler, groaning and becoming red-hot. The thirty-foot stack poured forth smoke and sparks. A man ran about with a pot of

In this old engraving, the Clermont *is shown using both sail and steam. Each artist seems to have drawn the ship to his own taste.*

molten lead, stopping up cracks in the boiler.

The *Clermont* shook and rumbled. Then she moved into midstream and went slowly up the river. She left a wild scene behind her. People trampled each other on shore. Sailors and bargemen thought that the devil was inside a ship that moved without sail and against the tide. Some people became so excited that they fell into the river.

On board the *Clermont* passengers sang and laughed. At the home of Mr. Livingston they went ashore for a feast and to celebrate the engagement of Harriet Livingston to Robert Fulton. The steamboat continued on up to Albany. It made the voyage in thirty-two hours. The return trip took only thirty. Two weeks later a steamboat was making regular runs on the Hudson River.

Robert Livingston knew when he had a good invention. He was a powerful man in New York State. He saw to it that a law was passed to keep other steamboats from operating unless they paid him a toll. Two New Jersey shipbuilders saw their steamboats destroyed by court order. Fulton built more steamers and made improvements in them.

There were some people in New Jersey, however, who wouldn't give up. After all, New Jersey owned part of the Hudson's shoreline. One day a tiny steamer called the *Mouse-of-the-Mountain* chugged and puffed her way from Elizabeth Town, New Jersey, to New York City. A New York court order was issued for the owner, but he did not come because he lived in New Jersey. So many people wanted to ride the *Mouse* that a new and larger steamboat, called the *Bellona*, was built. It had a captain of Dutch descent named Cornelius Vanderbilt.

When he docked at the southern tip of Manhattan, constables tried to catch him. But Vanderbilt was as slippery as a wet mackerel. After he grew tired of dodging the officers of the law, he had a hole built behind a secret panel in his cabin. There he crouched, laughing silently, while baffled constables searched for him.

New York courts were never able to catch Vanderbilt and put him in jail. By this time the whole country had read of the cat-and-mouse game on the Hudson River. They cheered for Captain Vanderbilt. The case came to the Supreme Court of the United

Troy from the west bank of the Hudson, 1837.

States. Daniel Webster spoke, and his deep voice seemed to boom across the land.

"The people of New York have a right to be protected against this monopoly."

Chief Justice Marshall and the Court decided that other people should be allowed to operate steamboats on the river. After that, shipyards were busy turning out more steamboats. New vessels, puffing up and down, put the old sailing sloops out of business, except for freight. Passengers loved steamboats and had their favorites. At each wharf employees drummed up trade for their boats. One steamboat became a showboat. Another was a theater for operatic concerts on the river. At night kerosene lamps and lanterns winked like stars on the water.

"Steamboat race! Around the point. Look at her go!"

Racing was dangerous. Boilers burst, and sometimes people were blown to bits. Steamboats often crashed together. Many passengers as well as crewmen were drowned in Hudson waves. This had to stop. *The New York Herald* started a campaign. It told people that the real reason for racing was commercial. It was competition for trade and publicity. A law was passed forbidding steamboat racing.

Now the river was safer, though less exciting. The queen of the river steamers was the *Mary Powell*, built in 1861. She was a trim and lovely boat. For 62 years she chugged along the Great River of the Mountains. She was always on time, and she never had a real rival.

From an oil painting of the steamboat Mary Powell *in 1861.*

"Ride on the *Mary Powell!* She'll get you there on time and in one piece. She has never lost a passenger!"

Eighteen years after the *Clermont's* historic trip, there was another great day on the Hudson. That was October 26, 1825. It was a crisp and golden day when everybody from Albany to Staten Island moved about as if listening for something. There it was! A distant cannon boomed out. It told New Yorkers and New Jerseyites that the Great Lakes and the Atlantic had been joined by the new Erie Canal.

71

On November 4, a procession of boats came down the Hudson towing decorated barges. Whistles, horns and rousing hurrahs greeted the boats and barges as they moved on to the Atlantic Ocean. There speeches were made, and the Governor of New York State poured a keg of Lake Erie water into the ocean.

The Erie Canal connected Lake Erie with other lakes and streams. It joined these to the Hudson River. Now passengers and freight could travel by water from the Atlantic, up the Hudson and the Mohawk, along the Erie Canal and into the Great Lakes. From there they could go west easily and more quickly than before.

Fulton's steamboat made it possible to open up the western land to settlers. The Erie Canal made New York harbor one of the great ports of the world. Now it sent the whole river valley into rapid growth.

When Washington Irving was a young man he often listened to river skippers' tales. He also rode along the Hudson's shores, gathering old stories to write into books. One of these was the tale of

Drawing by Aldren Watson

Ichabod Crane made a wild ride past Sleepy Hollow graveyard.

Ichabod Crane and his wild ride past the old grave-yard of Sleepy Hollow Church. This was called "The Legend of Sleepy Hollow." When people came to the river, they wanted to see the spot near Tarrytown where unhappy Ichabod met the fearful ghost of a Hessian soldier. It was on a bridge not far from the tree under which Major André had been captured.

Some of Irving's tales brought creepy shivers. Others were funny. But there was one that seemed to foretell the future ahead of Manhattan Island.

73

To Oloffe the clouds of smoke looked like "domes and lofty spires."

This was the story of Oloffe, the Dreamer, who lived in the time when New Amsterdam was a village. Drowsing beneath an oak, Oloffe beheld Saint Nicholas come down and sit beside him. As the good saint puffed on his Dutch pipe, smoke rose in clouds and took on wonderful shapes in the sky. To Oloffe they looked like "palaces and domes and lofty spires." We sometimes remember Oloffe's dream when we look at the New York skyline from across the river.

As the nineteenth century grew older, the hold

of the rich landlords grew weaker. At last, tenant farmers had the right to own land. Yet the patroon castles were still perched grandly on the heights above the Hudson River.

Other types of houses were built too. Some had cutout wooden decorations called "gingerbread." Others were eight-sided and were called Octagon houses, with some of their rooms shaped like slices of pie.

Many artists came to paint the magnificent scenery along the Hudson. They became famous as the Hudson River School of painting. West Point was made the U. S. Military Academy for training Army officers. And New York City became the financial center of the world.

The river was busy with ships and barges. For a while, even whaling boats sailed from Hudson River ports. Big stone buildings were built on the river banks for the storage of ice. In winter they received ice cut from the river. In summer the ice was towed on barges to the city. Cargo ships carried freight to Albany, and steamers plied the river constantly. Along the shores factories, quarries, brickyards and

The Battery of New York, 1847, from a painting by Samuel Waugh.

cement plants kept company with farms and vine-yards. Railroad trains puffed beside the river on both sides.

As New York City grew, ferryboats took passengers back and forth from New Jersey and Staten Island. The harbor was alive with ships from all over the world, and the New York shipyards were busy providing more vessels for American owners.

America was the Promised Land to Europeans. For many years they arrived by crowded shipload every day. The first American earth that they touched was tiny Ellis Island in New York harbor.

There the Immigration Office was located. Ellis Island is no longer an immigration station. But in the year 1907, one and a quarter million people passed through it into America.

October 28, 1886, was a cold, wet day. But thousands of New Yorkers jammed the waterfront. They were joined by visitors from many states and other lands. They saw a gray river filled with boats of every kind. Dripping flags of all nations flapped from the masts. On Bedloe's Island there was a huge bulk, covered by the French flag. As the flag dropped, a roar of whistles, naval guns and wild shouting greeted the misty face of the Statue of Liberty.

The Statue of Liberty stands on a tiny island in New York harbor.

Engraved inside the pedestal there is a poem written by Emma Lazarus. It includes these lines:

". . . . *Give me your tired, your poor,*
Your huddled masses yearning to breathe free,
The wretched refuse of your teeming shore.
Send these, the homeless, tempest-tost, to me:
I lift my lamp beside the golden door!"

The tall copper figure is 151 feet high. Her up-held torch is 305 feet above the waters of the Hudson River and the Bay. Inside of her head, one may stand to look out at the far-flung beauty of the River That Runs Two Ways.

☆ ☆ ☆

When the nineteenth century ended, people were calling the island city in the Hudson harbor, "Little Old New York." It was an exciting, energetic city that was always changing.

The Statue of Liberty was presented to the United States by the people of France in 1884.
New York State Department of Commerce

6. The City of Cloud Splitters

River shores also change as men cut, dig, blast, build and pave. Once the Great River of the Mountains was the only route from New York harbor to far places in the north and west. Once little villages tucked away in the hills seemed as distant as the homelands of the Dutch, French, English and Germans across the seas. Once sails were thick on the rippling river.

A long time before that dugouts and canoes made of hemlock bark were sent skimming on the water by Indian hands on paddles. Once there were tall forests crowning the high bluffs of the Palisades.

And once an island called Manhattan was green from the creek at Spuyten Duyvil to the Battery park.

No more river steamboats spurt water from their revolving paddles on regular runs to Albany and back. There are no more Dutch sloops to dip their peak sails in greeting to the Heer, with his sugarloaf hat and trumpet, on Thunder Mountain.

However, New Yorkers can still crowd on excursion boats on hot days. They go to Bear Mountain to camp or picnic. And in autumn, steamboats are used for special trips to West Point for football games.

Cars roll north and south beside the Hudson, bringing people from everywhere to see the sights. There is the town of Glens Falls, where the tumbling water of the Hudson makes power for factories. There is Albany, the capital on a hill. Castles, mansions and the houses of the mighty are now turned into schools, hospitals and church buildings. Only a few of the descendants of Dutch patroons and English landlords remain on their old estates.

Some of the old houses in Hudson Town still hug the river bank. They seem to be watching for whalers to come sailing in with the tide and a following wind.

And as a freighter sails down river in springtime, seamen sniff scented breezes blowing from Rhinebeck, where acres of violets are grown.

Artists from the colony in Woodstock, in the Catskill Mountains, come often to Saugerties, on the river's west bank. They like to paint pictures of the colorful town. Near here the enormous Ashokan Reservoir collects mountain streams and pours them through pipes for New Yorkers.

At Hyde Park, on the eastern shore, one estate is a National Shrine. This is the Franklin Delano Roosevelt home. Visitors wander about the mansion to see some of the Roosevelt possessions. They look at a black cloak, rows of well-used books and models of ships. They see a wheel chair, where President Roosevelt once sat to guide his country on a stormy sea of war.

The river itself is unchanged as it flows from Mt. Marcy to the ocean. Yet on its surface, beside it, beneath it and above it, there are a great number of changes. In fact, there are enough changes to take the breath from a fat Dutchman of old New Amsterdam.

Sunnyside, *the home of Washington Irving, is now open to visitors.*

There are a number of bridges on the upper Hudson. In the Highlands a high bridge connects Bear Mountain with Anthony's Nose. From this point of land the road winds down through tree-shaded towns. It goes past grim Sing Sing Prison at Ossining and on into Tarrytown. There the home of Washington Irving is maintained for visitors to see. The house is a vast collection of quaint gables having as many "angles and corners as an old cocked hat," according to Irving.

83

The salty waters of the lower Hudson are always moving with tides and winds, rain and bright breezes. The river is a place for races, regattas and outboard motor recreation. On the western shore the Palisades were in danger of complete ruin just after the turn of the century. Men were gouging out quarries and removing loads of gravel and stone. They blasted away headlands and cut the big trees. A campaign was begun by citizens of both states. They saved these impressive cliffs and preserved some of the forests for parks.

Below the Highlands a new bridge spans the wide Tappan Zee, connecting Nyack to Tarrytown. Farther down river nets and poles still appear in springtime alongside the channel, where freighters, yachts and naval vessels are anchored. Fishermen haul in their catch of silver-scaled shad.

High above the nets, the George Washington Bridge joins Fort Lee to Fort Washington Heights. It is one of the three longest suspension bridges in the world. It has also been called the most beautiful of all bridges. Under the bridge, on Jeffrey's Hook, a little red lighthouse still stands. Although its

Port of New York Authority

The George Washington Bridge and the little red lighthouse.

light no longer burns, it has been kept there for children, who love it.

When a fire blazes on the waterfront, fireboats scoot through lanes of river traffic to shoot streams of water on shore. Harbor police boats patrol the river too. There is constant movement here.

Luxury liners are nosed into their berths by busy little tugs. Here comes the huge steamship, the *United States!* And the *Queen Elizabeth!* Other giant liners from every country arrive and depart.

The Queen Elizabeth *coming into New York harbor.*

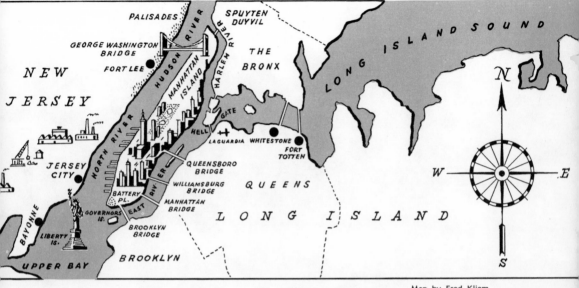

Map by Fred Kliem

Little sightseeing boats circle Manhattan in summer, unafraid of the Spuyten Duyvil, or the Hell Gate Spook.

Beneath the waves of the Hudson there are tunnels for railroads and for automobiles. Thousands of cars move into and out of Manhattan every day through the Lincoln and Holland tunnels.

Overhead the sun glistens on silver wings of airplanes. The roar of a jet outdistancing its sound is not surprising any more. As planes wing past at night, the sky twinkles with red and white lights

87

Above: Passengers on the Staten Island ferry study the skyline.
Left: A tugboat guides coal barges through New York harbor.

flashing among the stars. Helicopters circle over the George Washington Bridge, watching long lines of cars. And, now and then, the harbor seems to explode with fireworks and noise as the river puts on a celebration.

Along Hudson roads, a tide of cars moves by day and by night where bicyclists used to ride. Most of the old ferries have gone to some graveyard of the river. Yet the Jersey City ferry still runs. And

Standard Oil Co. (N. J.) photos

Railroad yards on the Jersey shore are piled high with freight.

Staten Island ferry boats continue to bump their pilings.

Little Old New York is no longer little. Its population makes it the third largest city in the world. In its canyon streets there are whole cities of foreign-speaking people from every place in the world.

New York never seems old either. It is always changing, always tearing down, always rebuilding! High structures of glass and steel seem to rise over-

90

Wall Street runs like a narrow canyon
across lower Manhattan.

United Nations buildings border the East River in mid-Manhattan.

night. Broadway—once a little tree-shaded road—
is now one of the longest streets in the world. At
night it glows with fantastic lights.

Thirteen miles by two-and-a-half! That is the size
of Manhattan Island. Since the city could not grow
outward into the Hudson River, it went straight up
instead. While subways were being cut into the rock
below, skyscrapers were going up above. They
tower and climb into the sky, in points and oblongs
and in terraces.

The Hudson River, born on the slope of Cloud Splitter Mountain, ends at the City of Cloud Splitters. The little green island where Oloffe had his dream is no more. "Little Old New York" of sixty years ago has also disappeared into the pages of books. But Oloffe's dream has come true. Changes come and go again. Yet Henry Hudson's Great River of the Mountains never really changes. It flows along in its deep channel until it is lost in the rolling waves of the Atlantic.

Tugboats keep traffic moving on the lower Hudson River.

Index

Meet the Author

MAY McNEER has become one of the best-known writers of regional and historical books for young readers in the United States. She has written biographies—*John Wesley*, *America's Abraham Lincoln* and *War Chief of the Seminoles*, among others. She has written of historical events—*The California Gold Rush* and *The Alaska Gold Rush*, for example. And she has written regional books of fiction and nonfiction such as *The Story of the Southwest* and *Little Baptiste*.

She is the winner of the Thomas Alva Edison Award and on several occasions has received the Boys' Clubs of America Award. On many books she has collaborated with her husband, Lynd Ward, the distinguished artist.

May McNeer was born in Tampa, Florida, and graduated from the Pulitzer School of Journalism at Columbia University. The Wards live in Cresskill, New Jersey, a suburb of New York. Their summer home is in the Canadian woods, the scene of *Little Baptiste*.